PRAISE FOR
101 CHUCK YEAGER-ISMS

"I was blessed as an Air Force Fighter Pilot and Test Pilot to have known and flown with General Yeager in a variety of aircraft over many years. His witty and insightful comments conveyed a mix of humor, candor/directness and experience that this book captures incredibly well and brings to life. I see my role model, mentor and friend in these pages and know you'll enjoy getting to know him a little better as you read these great stories, too!"

—Col. Pat Duffy USAF (ret.), Test Pilot & IP
with General Yeager in F-15, F-16, F-18

"Such a great tribute to 'General Chuck', a man I admired and knew very well for over 35 years! He and I took part in many special events together during my 40-year Airshow career and nearly 30 years flying for Northwest Airlines where General Chuck personally represented the airline in safety issues. I grew to realize his true insightfulness and very quick wit. Such an extraordinary man!!! This book, so lovingly put together by Victoria, just tells the true "character" of a great mind and man. He may have taken great risks, but these 'Yeager-isms' really tell the story of what a brilliant mind he had to stay alive and 'fly the airplane!!'"

—Capt. Julie E. Clark NWA (ret), Award-winning
Airshow performer (41 years) T-34/T-28

i

"Here it is: the wit, wisdom and astonish-
ing courage of a great American hero.
As he said: 'Everyone's got a job to do,
son.' He did his, superlatively well, and
Victoria Yeager tells us about it in the
pilot's own words. Read it, learn and be
inspired."

—Rabbi David Wolpe, named the Most Influential Rabbi
in America by Newsweek and one of the 50 Most
Influential Jews in the World by The Jerusalem Post

"This book brought tears and joy as it
elicited so many great memories. We
so loved this man...Thank you, Chuck
Yeager, for enriching our lives. Rest
Easy in the Everlasting Arms, General,
until the promised day when we will
gather once again to sing for you and to hear your jokes and stories. You, Sir, represented the BEST of ALL of us!"

—Joe Bonsall/Oak Ridge Boys

"I served under Colonel Chuck Yeager's command as a student and staff member at the
USAF test pilot school. He was a demanding
but fair boss whom I deeply respected and
admired. General Yeager, my mentor, comes
alive in these pages of great wisdom and
humor from vast experience, not only for pilots and astronauts,
but for everyone."

—Brig. Gen. Charlie Duke, USAF (ret.),
Lunar Module Pilot, Apollo 16, astronaut

"Several years ago, I had the great pleasure of meeting General Yeager and Victoria at a hunters' convention. I will admit to having been more than a little awestruck at meeting a genuine childhood hero. Truth be told, I still am. Since that time, I have been honoured to call them friends.

"Almost everyone knows something about the exploits of the greatest aviator of them all. A few of us got to know the humour of this great man. This book will let those not lucky enough to have known him get a glimpse at the wit and wisdom of the man from West Virginia who changed the world through his work and made it a better place just by being in it. Meet my friend Chuck Yeager."

—Gerald "Mac" McRaney, actor, outdoorsman

"I first met Colonel Chuck Yeager when we filmed 'I Dream of Jeanie' at Edwards AFB, CA. His charm, wit, and sense of fun come through beautifully in this book."

—Barbara Eden, singer, actress, author, producer

"Chuck Yeager was the Ace of Aces. He challenged the demons that lived in the air and was the first to poke a hole in the sky. The heavens were his battle-ground, but he was also the most down-to-earth guy you could ever meet. He was a steely-eyed straight shooter who didn't mince words or suffer fools when it came to getting the job done right. He was also a twinkly-eyed, fun-loving guy who truly understood what the Pursuit of Happiness was all about. Thanks to Victoria Yeager, we now have this book of his wit and wisdom to remind us that he is still up there somewhere, doing what he always did."

—Philip Kaufman, writer, director (*The Right Stuff*)

101 Chuck YEAGER-isms

Wit & Wisdom from America's Hero, The Right Stuff

By New York Times #1 best-selling author
GENERAL CHUCK YEAGER
and his favorite wingman VICTORIA YEAGER

General Chuck Yeager flying F-15E, Edwards AFB, CA

101 Chuck YEAGER-isms
Wit & Wisdom from America's Hero, The Right Stuff

Authors: General Charles E. "Chuck" Yeager & Victoria Yeager

Publisher:

THE RIGHT STUFF
PUBLISHING

The Right Stuff Publishing

Book cover art: Stu Shepherd
Book cover & interior layout: TeaBerryCreative.com

ISBN: (paperback) 979-8-8490446-7-5
ISBN: (hardcover) 979-8-8490496-7-0
ISBN: (eBook) 979-8-9864982-1-8

This book is dedicated to General Charles E. "Chuck" Yeager;
his parents, Hal, Sr. & Susie Mae Yeager;
his older brother Roy; and Grandpa (Marion General) Yeager;
all of whom taught and raised him well.

Roy Yeager, Susie Mae Yeager, Hal Yeager, Chuck Yeager

This book is also dedicated to General Ben Davis, Jr., General Jimmy
Doolittle, Major General Al Boyd, Colonel Jack Ridley, and all General
Chuck Yeager's wingmen, IPs, and maintainers; who kept him safe.

Chuck Yeager in F-86D (U.S. Air Force)

CONTENTS

General Chuck Yeager
(1975 retirement from active duty)
and Flight Officer Yeager,
(U.S. Air Force)

GENERAL CHUCK YEAGER
BIOGRAPHY

Charles E. "Chuck" Yeager, America's hero and the most righteous of The Right Stuff, is one of the greatest aviators that ever lived. His commitment to service, duty, courage, and love of his country and its flag are evident in all that he did during active duty and beyond. He was, and continues to be, a great inspiration and role model to people the world over.

Born in Hamlin, West Virginia, on February 13, 1923, Yeager enlisted in the Army Air Corps in September 1941, at the age of eighteen. In July 1942, he was accepted for pilot training under the flying sergeant program. He received his pilot wings and appointment as a flight officer in March 1943.

During World War II, with his exceptional eyesight and hand-eye coordination, Yeager distinguished himself in aerial combat over France and Germany by shooting down at least 13 enemy aircraft. On March 5, 1944, he was shot down over German-occupied France but evaded capture with the help of the French Underground. In turn, Yeager helped the Maquis (French Resistance) put together explosives and then escaped over the most challenging, steepest region of the Pyrenees in three feet of snow and freezing cold weather, carrying a wounded airman.

When Yeager returned to England, he was ordered home. He refused and fought this order all the way up the chain of command to General Eisenhower, the Supreme Allied Commander, who said, "I don't normally see guys like you, but I am curious. I've got people shooting themselves in the foot to go home; what's the matter with you?"

Yeager replied, "I haven't done my job."

Ultimately, after D-Day, June 6, 1944, the Maquis rose up out of the shadows and fought openly, and Yeager was allowed back on combat. Four months later, Yeager achieved "ace in a day" status and was also the first in his squadron to shoot down one of Germany's much faster jets from his P-51 Mustang, a propeller plane.

He returned to West Virginia a war hero celebrated with a parade and more.

But he was just getting started.

In February 1945, Yeager married Glennis Dickhouse. They had four children and remained together until her passing in 1990.

In 1947, Yeager was selected to fly the X-1 and attempt to break the sound barrier, which he achieved on October 14, 1947, at a speed of 1.06 Mach.

When he left Edwards AFB, CA in 1954 to eventually become the commander of the 417th Fighter Squadron at Hahn Air Base, Germany, he was already a legend, yet he continued to embody exceptionalism.

He then alternated between fighter squadrons and test squadrons. From 1961 to 1966, he trained the early astronauts. Then, from 1966 to 1973, he commanded fighter wings in Vietnam, Germany, and Pakistan. From 1973-1975, he was Director of Safety for the Air Force.

Yeager retired from active military duty in 1975 but continued to consult for the Air Force, flying most of their airplanes.

Yeager also worked on various movies, including *The Right Stuff,* created a computer game, wrote two books, and more. His book, *Yeager, An Autobiography,* #1 on the *New York Times* best-seller list for over five months, sold over 1.2 million copies. The movie, *The Right Stuff*, was, in part, based on his own story.

The numerous military decorations and awards General Yeager received include the Distinguished Service Medal, Silver Star with oak leaf cluster, Legion of Merit with oak leaf cluster, Distinguished Flying Cross with two oak leaf clusters, Bronze Star Medal with "V" device, Air Medal with ten oak leaf clusters, Air Force Commendation Medal, Purple Heart, Distinguished Unit Citation Emblem with oak leaf cluster, and the Air Force Outstanding Unit Award Ribbon. He was a command pilot and flew more than 12,000 hours in 361 different makes and models of military aircraft all around the world.

General Chuck Yeager flying F-15E,
Edwards AFB, CA 1997 (U.S. Air Force)

By special act of Congress (making it one of the rare true Congressional Medals of Honor), General Yeager was awarded the Special Silver Congressional Medal of Honor (essentially a peacetime Medal of Honor) in 1976.

US President Ronald Reagan presented General Chuck Yeager with the highest civilian award, the Presidential Medal of Freedom, in 1985. In 2003, France bestowed on General Yeager the rank of Officer of their Legion of Honor, the highest award for a non-citizen. Congress also awarded General Yeager, for his accomplishments as a World War II fighter ace, the Gold Congressional Medal.

Chuck Yeager met Victoria, a non-profit and financial consultant, writer, producer, and actor, in 2000. They married in 2003. He taught her how to fly, hunt, and fish, among other things.

The truth is that General Chuck Yeager was an extraordinary man in private as well as in public. His father told him after he broke the sound barrier and gained stature, "Never forget where you came from, Son." And Chuck Yeager never did.

America and the world over will cherish always the memory, the service, and the example of General Chuck Yeager.

INTRODUCTION
BY VICTORIA YEAGER

When I went hiking that spring day in March 2000, in the foot-
hills of the High Sierra, to commune with the miracle of nature,
enjoy the beautiful spring wildflowers and magnificent, crisp, clear
sunny day, little did I know that a chance meeting would change my
already interesting, yet solitary, life exponentially for the better. As
I was walking up the hill on a trail where I rarely saw anyone else;
a handsome, fit, older man was walking down. The sun was behind
him, creating an ethereal radiance. Or maybe it was just his lovely,
contagious smile and exquisite blue-green eyes. I saw blue; he said
green. General Charles "Chuck" Yeager.

General Charles E. "Chuck" Yeager & Victoria
Nellis AFB October 14, 2012 (U.S. Air Force)

For the next 20+ years, we laughed a lot, we cried a little, we loved deeply, enjoyed many, many grand adventures together, and effortlessly lived those vows to love, honor, cherish, be faithful, in sickness and in health, for richer, for poorer, till death do us part; from long before we were married. My real man kept me safe, warm, and very loved for the rest of his life. And then some.

Thank you, Charlie. I love you so.

Join me now, as we share Chuck Yeager's great wit and wisdom.

Chapter 1
LIFE LESSONS

NO. OO1

"You don't have to be good to be a legend, all you gotta do is live."

NO. 002

"I was born so fer
('far' in West Virginian)
up a holler, they had
to pipe daylight in."

NO. 003

"An arrogant pilot will get ya killed; confident ones make history."

During combat in World War II, Flight Officer Yeager often led the 357th Fighter Group. After a successful dogfight, Flight Officer (F/O) Yeager was leading a flight of four back to Leiston, their base in England. Tail End Charlie (the last aircraft in a flying formation) was dropping far behind. Yeager told him to move into close formation. The arrogant pilot, a college graduate with a rank senior to Yeager's, refused. So, Yeager did a barrel roll, got behind him, and shot some tracers over the belligerent pilot's wing. That pilot formed up right quick. As soon as they landed at Leiston air base, the condescending pilot tried to get Yeager court-martialed, but the Commanding Officer said, "I would have done the same thing!"

Trailing so far behind, that pilot could have been easily picked off by enemy aircraft; thus, jeopardizing the whole flight.

NO. 004

During World War II, in the Nissen huts at Leiston air base in England, there were four or more to a hut.

"If a guy was snoring, you go kiss him full on the lips. He'd stay up all night staring at you."

"And the rest of us could get some sleep."

NO. 005

"I fought wars with less of a briefing."

The Canadian Air Force Demonstration Team, the Snowbirds, will take a full hour to go through their entire routine verbally in their chairs. This was Yeager's quip after he witnessed this.

NO. 006

"When the paperwork weighs more than the airplane, you're ready to fly."

NO. 007

"If everything is going well, check six."

The ebb and flow of life. "Check six" refers to a clock. 12 is straight ahead, six is behind. "Check six" means look behind you at what's there or approaching.

NO. 008

"Rules are made for those unwilling to make up their own—but you better be right!"

A lot of people don't understand this Chuck Yeager-ism: "Rules are made for those unwilling to make up their own." Many commanders who had asked General Yeager to speak groaned when they heard this. What they failed to remember, and continue to fail to remember, is the last line: "But you better be right!" Then it makes more sense and shows great wisdom, as General Yeager did in this story:

Chuck Yeager: "For me, the craziest part of Vietnam was back at Clark Air Base."

During the Vietnam war, Yeager was based at Clark Air Base in the Philippines. The head of the Thirteenth Air Force was a General Jim Wilson, who scared everyone, including Yeager. Wilson had a policy that airplanes would be scheduled for maintenance based on the plane's tail number.

Because of this, Yeager was expected to predict a month in advance when a certain aircraft would need maintenance, even in the middle of a war, even though an aircraft could be shot out of the sky or otherwise put out of service at any moment. Obviously, the schedule should change. But it didn't.

"But, Sir, that plane was shot down last month!"

General Wilson, a stickler for details and strict adherence to his orders, didn't care. He would watch from the taxi strip with a master list in hand, reading off planes' tail numbers as they taxied past him. If the tail numbers of the planes shooting past didn't correspond to the numbers on his list, Wilson went ballistic.

This drove Yeager nuts, until he and another colonel, Eddie White, came up with an ingenious plan. They repainted a plane's tail number to conform to Wilson's master list before the plane left the maintenance hangar to be reviewed by Wilson.

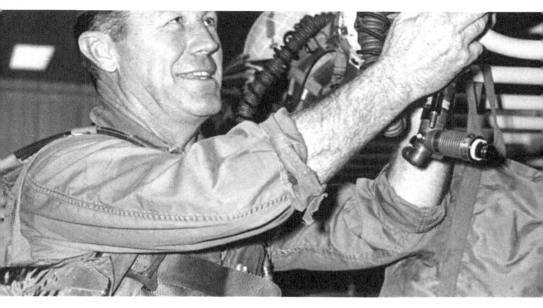

Colonel Charles E. "Chuck" Yeager
Clark AFB, Philippines 1966-68
(U.S. Air Force)

General Wilson was none the wiser, and, in fact, later gave Yeager one of the best officer-effectiveness reports he ever received.

In Yeager's own words: **"I'm sure the records never did get straightened out, but I got out of there with my whole skin!"**

NO. 009

"Find out what you like to do (for a living) and make your lifestyle fit your income, not the other way around."

You spend most of your life working, so you might as well do something you enjoy.

Some try to make a lot of money to have a better lifestyle, but in making that money, they don't have time to enjoy it.

NO. 010

"Everybody that I've ever seen that enjoyed their job was very good at it."

Most people like what they are good at and will do a better job if they like it. They will also feel good about themselves.

NO. 011

"In the end, or at the moment of truth, there are only excuses or results."

NO. 012

"You gotta have fun in life. Whatever I did, I always included fun."

"Unfortunately, many people do not consider fun an important item on their daily agenda. For me, that was always a high priority in whatever I was doing."

Even while Chuck Yeager was in England going on sorties, dog-fightin', fightin' a war, or, as he would say, "being shot at, shot down, or shot up"; back at base, he was a prankster although this one actually happened while training for combat in Caspar, WY: One particularly freezing cold day, Yeager walked into the drafty barracks where four of the flight leaders, including Yeager, slept. They had their pot belly coke (coal-based fuel) stove heating the hut. Yeager sauntered in, walked up to the stove as though he were carrying a handful of coal, opened the stove door, threw in what he was actually carrying (50 caliber bullets), shut the door, and rushed out. A few seconds later, just as the other three were real-izing something was afoot, bang bang bang bang– bullets started discharging within the coke stove– the other three guys ducked for cover. (No one was hurt; the discharge stayed within the solid pot belly stove, which Yeager knew would happen.)

NO. 013

"Duty."

"You've got a job to do, you do it, especially in the military. When I was picked to fly the X-1, it was my duty to fly it, and I did."

"The one word you use in military flying is 'Duty'. It's your duty. You have no control over the outcome. No control over pick and choose. It's duty."

"Duty" was also Yeager's answer to General Dwight Eisenhower, the Supreme Allied Commander in Europe during World War II.

After Yeager had been shot down and made his way back to England by evading the Germans and fleeing across the Pyrenees, he was scheduled to be sent home. The fear was that if Yeager were shot down again and captured by the Germans, he might break under torture and reveal classified information about the French Underground. But Yeager wanted to keep fighting, so he worked his way up the ladder until he reached the very top: General Eisenhower.

General Eisenhower met with Flight Officer Yeager and another evadee. The General asked Yeager, "I normally don't meet with guys like you, but I was curious. I've got people shooting themselves in the foot to go home. Why don't you want to go home?"

Yeager replied, "Sir, you've spent all this time training me and I haven't done my job yet. Duty."

General Eisenhower knew D-Day was coming when all those in the French Resistance would rise up out of the shadows and fight openly. Keeping this classified information secret, General Eisenhower merely said he had to get permission from Washington, DC, and sent Yeager back to his base to await word on whether he could return to combat.

On combat four months later, Yeager attained "ace in a day" status. The *Stars and Stripes* newspaper headline was: "Flyer Bags 5 Nazi Planes to Vindicate Ike's Ruling". Later, Yeager was the first in his group to shoot down a German jet, the Me 262, from his P-51 Mustang, a propeller plane.

Flier Bags 5 Nazi Planes To Vindicate Ike's Ruling

A ruling by Gen. Eisenhower last July cancelling the orders which would have returned 1/Lt. Charles E. Yeager, Mustang pilot from Hamlin, W. Va., to the U.S. after being shot down and wounded in enemy territory and getting back to England proved to be bad news for the Luftwaffe.

The 21-year-old squadron leader, who holds the distinction of having led his group while still holding the rank of flight officer, last Thursday bagged five Messerschmitt 109s over Bremen. Although his original claim was four enemy craft destroyed, the fifth kill was confirmed by other pilots in his squadron who had seen the German plane crash.

Yeager was wounded in action over Berlin last March. Recovered, he was determined to seek revenge on the Luftwaffe and went to Eisenhower for permission to return to action.

"I had to go through a lot of channels to see Gen. Ike," he related. "I went from one office to another and from one high officer to another, until I found myself in front of his desk."

Yeager's recent victories brought his official score to seven.

1/Lt. Charles E. Yeager

(Artwork by Stu Shepherd)

a. Corollary: "It's your duty to fly the airplane. If you get killed you don't know anything about it anyway. Duty is paramount. It's that simple."

General Yeager was often called on to train other outfits. One such bomber outfit was missing its target out of fear. He instructed them that they had signed up to be in the military. "Duty. Do your job and do it well."

NO. 014

"You do what you can for as long as you can. And when you finally can't, you do the next best thing; you back up, but you don't give up."

This applies to life. Said slightly differently: "When you can no longer do the thing you love to do, you back up and you do the next best thing."

Yeager chose to stop flying the P-51 Mustang at age 89. "These planes are old–70 years old." He just didn't want to have to jump (parachute) out of another airplane. So, he flew more modern planes—taildraggers, jets, and others.

General Chuck Yeager piloting an F-16
(U.S. Air Force)

NO. 015

"Complacency will kill you."

For pilots:

"Complacency is when the plane bites the hardest."

General Yeager's friend had flown a P-51 Mustang to Edwards AFB, California for its airshow. Yeager had the parachute packing experts at Edwards AFB, check the parachutes before his friend and he were going to fly. The friend insisted the parachutes were fine. Yeager still had them checked, which turned out to be very wise. The parachutes had been badly folded and packed. If needed and without the re-packing, the pilot and his passenger would have perished relying on those parachutes.

NO. 016

"If you want to test a person's character, give them a little bit of authority."

When Chuck Yeager was given power, he picked the best people to work for him, let them do their jobs, and gave them credit. He told them, "If it looks like any of you might make mistakes I have already made, I will warn you so you won't make those same mistakes." That's extreme wisdom—learning from others' mistakes.

NO. 017

"Always leave yourself a way out."

For instance, whenever General Yeager was flying, he always tracked and knew, at any second, ahead of time, where he would land if his airplane's engine failed.

In World War II, after Yeager was shot down and was protected by the Maquis (French Resistance), he often went off on his own on a bicycle to explore escape routes and hiding places. He knew he had to rely on himself as much as possible.

NO. 018

"Situational awareness"

General Yeager always knew what was surrounding him and what was coming from all directions whether in an airplane or a car.

Be aware of your surroundings. Especially keep vigilant and be aware of obstacles, hazards, bogeys (unknown whether friend or foe), and bandits (bad guys).

And "Check six!"

NO. 019

"Don't miss the tanker."

(In other words, don't be late. In fact, be early. If you miss the tanker, you'll run out of fuel and fall from the sky. "And that's bad.")

Yeager: "When Colonel (Al) Boyd said, '8 am,' he meant wheels up at 8 am. If you weren't there early enough to be flying by 8 am, you got left behind. And you only ever did that once, if that."

Colonel Al Boyd, ultimately attaining the rank of Major General, was highly respected by the men and women under his command. He was Chief of the Maintenance Division at Wright Field, Ohio, then Chief of the Flight Test Division at Wright Patterson, Ohio, and eventually the Commanding Officer of the Air Force Flight Test Center at Edwards AFB, California. He was also an excellent experimental test pilot himself.

NO. 020

"You learn very fast in life when you're involved in the college of life and death, death doesn't mean a helluva lot to ya.

Hell, if it's a close call and it kills you, you're not around to talk about it anyway.

And if it didn't kill you, what the hell difference does it make?"

NO. 021

"Press on!"

When life knocks you down, and it will, because it knocks every-one down: Pick yourself up, dust yourself off, and keep moving forward. Press on.

NO. 022

"Those that do it on their own are the best."

a. Corollary: "Self-sufficiency works better for me than valium would."

General Yeager received all sorts of requests for a leg up artificially instead of on the person's own merits. He declined and would tell them this: "Those that do it on their own are the best." The confidence and sense of accomplishment that come from achieving on one's own are priceless.

NO. 023

On politics, especially while dining:

"Quit talkin' politics! You're giving me indigestion."

General Yeager had been exposed plenty to politics.

There was a struggle between the towns of Hubball, West Virginia, where young Charles "Chuck" Yeager spent ages 1-3 approximately, and Hamlin, West Virginia, where he spent the rest of his youth; as to which would be the county seat. Hamlin won out—it had more powerful people with more money to buy the politicians and the votes.

On election day, growing up in Hamlin, WV; young Charles Yeager witnessed several men giving out $2 bills and whiskey for votes.

The Robert J. Collier Trophy is an annual aviation award administered by the U.S. National Aeronautic Association (NAA), presented to those who have made "the greatest achievement in aeronautics or astronautics in America".

In 1948, when US President Harry S. Truman presented the Collier Trophy to Captain Yeager for his achievement in breaking the sound barrier the year before, Captain Yeager's father refused to shake that Democrat's (or any Democrat's) hand. Hal, Sr, stood in the corner, arms crossed, glaring at President

Truman. To cover, Chuck's mother, Susie Mae, exchanged corn-bread recipes with the President. U.S. Air Force Secretary Stuart Symington and General Hoyt Vandenburg, Chief of Staff of the Air Force, saw all this and fought against the giggles. After the Yeagers left the Oval Office, Susie Mae royally chewed Hal, Sr. out.

US President Harry S. Truman awarding
Captain Chuck Yeager the Collier Trophy, December 1948

After Captain Yeager broke the sound barrier and news leaked out, every politician in Washington, DC and across the nation wanted him as a speaker. He preferred to fly airplanes and do his job but the U.S. Air Force ordered him to do the speaking engagements. Yeager would be at a dinner, and some politician, smoking a cigar, would lean over to him, blow smoke, and ask, "What are you famous for? I'm supposed to be introducing you." It got old.

After General Yeager retired from active duty in the U.S. Air Force, several powerful people wanted him to run for Governor or Senator of West Virginia, or even President of the United States. General Yeager always polled at 95% or more against the competition. Yeager's answer was always an emphatic version of "No!"

Chapter 2

FAMILY—GROWING UP IN WEST VIRGINIA

*Front row: Roy (Chuck's older brother), Charles ("Chuck") Yeager,
Uncle Richard. (baby unknown)
(Courtesy of Victoria Yeager)*

NO. 024

"Growing up in West Virginia, I got saved two or three times a day

(by traveling preachers coming through town selling 'snake oil')."

NO. 025

"In West Virginia, people didn't have sex standing up because people might think they were dancing."

NO. 026

"We were so poor; we didn't know there was a Depression."

General Yeager, who was born in 1923 and who grew up in Hamlin, West Virginia, was speaking about the Great Depression, a severe worldwide depression that lasted from 1929 to 1939 after the 1929 stock market crash.

NO. 027

"There wasn't a pigeon in Hamlin till they erected a statue of me."

General Yeager said this at the ceremony for the unveiling of his statue in Hamlin, WV.

*1987: General Chuck Yeager in front of his statue in front of
Hamlin middle school, formerly Hamlin High: Hamlin, WV
(Photo by & courtesy of Steven Wayne Rotsch)*

Chapter 3
FLYING

NO. 028

"Most pilots learn when they pin on their wings and go out and get in a fighter especially, that one thing you don't do: you don't believe anything anybody tells you about an airplane."

General Yeager always told Victoria after she obtained her pilot's license;

"Learn to fly the plane your way."

NO. 029

"Any landing you can walk away from is a good landing. Any landing where you can use the plane the next day is an excellent landing."

NO. 030

"You may touch, but you ain't gonna go."

Neil Armstrong may have been the first man on the moon, but he wasn't prone to taking advice from a military pilot. Chuck Yeager was asked to act as co-pilot in the back seat of the X-15 with Neil flying as pilot in command. Neil wanted to practice emergency landings on Smith's Ranch Lake in preparation for his moon landing (the first ever). Chuck had recently flown over the area and knew it was still wet from winter rains, but Paul Bikle, head of NACA (precursor to NASA) at Edwards AFB, CA, said his guys insisted it was dry.

Chuck tried to talk Neil out of going, but Neil insisted, saying he wouldn't land, he just wanted to see it. Paul Bikle asked Chuck to go as a favor to Paul. Chuck acquiesced as long as he wasn't held responsible.

As Neil and Chuck flew over Smith's Ranch Lake, Neil said he was going to do a touch and go, meaning just set down the wheels for a moment, then hit the throttle and take off again.

Chuck replied, "You may touch, but you ain't gonna go."

And that's exactly what happened. The aircraft touched down, the wheels got stuck in the mud, and they could not take off again. Chuck said to Neil, "What are you going to do now?" They only had their summer flying suits on and it would get mighty cold come nightfall.

Bikle was smart enough to believe Chuck and had NACA send a Gooney Bird (D-3) to rescue Chuck and Neil. Chuck radioed the Gooney Bird pilot to give Neil and him time to walk the mile to the edge of the lake. Then the pilot should touch down on the edge, where it was drier, and keep rolling. Chuck and Neil would jump in.

When they got back to Edwards AFB, Bikle, still there waiting, burst out laughing when he saw Chuck.

Neil Armstrong, first man on the moon (1969), and Chuck Yeager, first man to fly faster than sound (1947) (Photo by Victoria Yeager 2012)

Yeager and Armstrong stuck in the mud: Smith Ranch Lake (1960s)

NO. 031

"Be my guest."

General Yeager said this whenever someone didn't take his advice, especially re flying. (The "someone" was always wrong to his/her detriment.)

One example is: Yeager was turning over the F-100 to NASA pilot Scott Crossfield for further testing.

F-100 (Artwork courtesy of Stu Shepherd)

Yeager told Crossfield, "When do you want me to check you out on the systems?" Crossfield, a college graduate, arrogantly replied, "It's got a pilot's handbook, doesn't it?"

Yeager said, "Be my guest," and walked off.

On his next flight, Crossfield lost his hydraulics, didn't know what to do, and couldn't stop the plane so he went up the ramp into the F-100 hangar, took out two F-100s, and damaged the hangar wall: All because he wouldn't listen to Yeager. An in-house cartoon made the rounds with Colonel Yeager saying: "The sonic wall is mine; the hangar wall is Crossfield's."

Dryden Flight Research Center E-1366 Photographed 1954
F-100 protruding through the hangar wall following
Scott Crossfield's emergency landing. NASA photo

Another example is: After advising the Israeli Air Force pilots on strategy, the Israeli pilots retorted they knew what they were doing and that General Yeager was "Vietnam-ized." General Yeager said,

"Be my guest," and walked off the stage.

The Israeli general chased after him and apologized for his arrogant fighter pilots. General Yeager told the Israeli general in no uncertain terms: "You're going to lose a lot of your aircraft with their attitude."

General Yeager was right: Israel did lose over 25% of their fighters in just three (3) weeks and the US had to re-supply them in the Israeli-Arab war.

NO. 032

"There's no such thing as a natural-born pilot. It takes hard work!"

"There is no such thing as a natural-born pilot. Whatever my aptitudes or talents, becoming a proficient pilot was hard work, really a lifetime's learning experience.

"For the best pilots, flying is an obsession, the one thing in life they must do continually. The best pilots fly more than the others; that's why they're the best."

NO. 033

"If there is such a thing as 'The Right Stuff', it's experience."

"Experience is everything. The eagerness to learn how and why every piece of equipment works is everything. And luck is everything, too."

NO. 034

"The most experienced pilots are the best— they've lived through their mistakes."

a. Corollary: "The best pilots are the ones that fly the most— experience."

Chuck Yeager: "I have flown in just about everything, with all kinds of pilots in all parts of the world— British, French, Italian, Pakistani, Iranian, Japanese, Chinese— and there wasn't a dime's worth of difference between any of them except for one unchanging, certain fact: the best, most skillful pilot has the most experience."

NO. 035

On his first airplane ride:

"Man, you made a big mistake!"

Chuck Yeager: "I was crew chief on an airplane and the pilot, knowing I had applied to pilot training, asked if I wanted to go for a ride. It was my first time in an airplane. After about thirty minutes, I puked all over my airplane (and had to clean it up myself!) I said to myself, 'Man, Yeager! You made a BIG mistake!' But I wasn't a quitter."

(U.S. Air Force)

NO. 036

"There ain't nothing that hasn't been done before, including making a smokin' hole in the ground."

a. Corollary: "There is no kind of ultimate goal to do something twice as good as anyone else can. The ultimate goal is just to do the job as best you can. If it turns out good, fine. If it doesn't, that's the way it goes."

This was his advice to pilots, especially hot-dog pilots.

NO. 037

"If you want to grow old as a pilot, you've got to know when to push it, and when to back off."

And General Chuck Yeager did grow old as a pilot. He lived to over ninety-seven years old: bucking the old adage, there are no old, bold pilots. Yes, there was at least one.

NO. 038

"The secret of my success is that I always managed to live to fly another day."

The object is to live and gain a lot of experience.

NO. 039

"Helicopters are 10,000 parts trying to fly apart!"

General Yeager was not fond of helicopters. He had flown many.

Colonel Yeager had a truly terrifying experience when a helicopter he was on crashed into a freezing lake. He'd spent a few days fishing with General Branch at the Rocky Basin Lakes, about 11,000 feet above sea level in the High Sierra. A Huey chopper came to pick them up to take them home, and they loaded up the craft with all their fish and other gear. The chopper engine froze and at 80 feet above the ground, the craft broke up and plunged inverted into the icy lake below. Everyone on board: pilot, co-pilot, crew chief, Colonel Yeager, and General Branch, were able to swim to shore.

General Branch, nicknamed "Twig", asked Chuck if he was okay. Chuck replied, "My head is burning. Why?"

Twig responded, "I can see your brains, for chrissake!" Chuck had a bad scalp injury that exposed the bone in five places and later required 138 sutures to close.

Twig headed out nine miles to the tunnel airstrip. Since Chuck was in good hiking shape and every time he lay down, he bled more; he also headed to the tunnel airstrip. When Twig saw Chuck emerge, his jaw dropped, thinking he was seeing Chuck's ghost.

"What the hell are you doing here?" Twig blurted out.

Chuck answered, "I got tired of standing around up there, so I walked out." As usual, Chuck relied on himself to get to safety.

General Chuck Yeager visiting troops in Afghanistan 2012
(Courtesy of Victoria Yeager)

NO. 040

On UFOs:

"I don't drink before I fly."

This was Yeager's response whenever he was asked if he had ever seen a UFO. He sometimes added, "I never saw something in the sky I didn't know what it was."

NO. 041

"Did ya learn anything?"

A friend called up to explain his airplane incident that had been on the news. Yeager cut him off; he didn't need to hear the ever-so-long saga and excuses (life is too short), so he interjected: "I know what happened. You were showing off, skipping on the water. Did ya learn anything?"

NO. 042

"Remember: the pilot arrives at the scene of the accident first."

Glennis: "I told Chuck I was nervous about his test work. Chuck said, 'Remember, I'm in the airplane.'"

Often civilian non-pilots would tell Chuck they were afraid to fly. Chuck would respond in jest: "Remember, the pilot always arrives at the scene of the accident first." They would all realize that statement made (common) sense so would become less nervous. It often worked.

NO. 043

"You fly the cockpit. The rest of the plane comes with you."

This was Yeager's response when others asked how he was able to fly the biggest civilian aircraft in the world for the first time.

Flight Officer Chuck Yeager with crew chief for his P-51
Leiston AB, World War II 1944
(U.S. Air Force)

Chapter 4
COMBAT

NO. 044

"The first time I saw a jet, I shot it down."

General Yeager was at a seminar where another fighter pilot was giving a long-winded description of how difficult it was trying to shoot down a jet.

When the other fighter pilot took a breath, the moderator turned to General Yeager, who immediately said: "First time I saw a jet, I shot it down."

Yeager proceeded to tell the story of being the first in his fighter group to shoot down a German jet, the Me 262. Yeager was flying a much slower propeller airplane, the P-51 Mustang.

Painting of Captain Chuck Yeager, in a P-51 Mustang, propeller aircraft, shooting down an Me 262 fighter jet. (Painting by Roy Grinnell; courtesy of American Fighter Aces, General Chuck Yeager & Victoria Yeager)

NO. 045

"The bigger a challenge you can make the opposition/enemy, the bigger a hero you are for hackin' it."

The other fighter pilot in the seminar (mentioned in preceding Yeager-ism) was giving a long-winded, detailed description of how difficult it was trying to shoot down a jet: They twisted and turned and switched places, back and forth, lost him, found him again...

When the blowhard was finished attempting to tell the story a second time, General Yeager interjected: "The bigger a challenge you can make the opposition/enemy, the bigger a hero you are for hackin' it." ("Hackin' it" is slang for handling or coping with a situation or an assignment adequately and calmly.)

NO. 046

"Unsportsmanlike, but what the hell?"

Captain Yeager, still on the European continent, making his way back in his P-51 Mustang to his base in England, saw an Me 262 (German jet) on final for landing. The Me 262's gear was down, and he was flying slowly: slowly enough for Yeager to catch up and shoot him down. As Yeager would say when recounting the story,

"Unsportsmanlike, but what the hell?"

Yeager's only egress was to fly low down the runway. The Germans were shooting at him, but the shots were going just over the canopy and damaging the other side of the Germans' own air base.

After Yeager got past the end of the runway, he flew straight up and got the heck out of there.

NO. 047

"Never make a second pass."

When asked why Yeager didn't go back and strafe the field after shooting down the Me 262 (mentioned in preceding Yeager-ism), General Yeager said, "And give them a second chance to shoot me down?!?!

"It's the bombers at the end of the bomb run that get shot down the most often because by then, the Germans are ready for 'em."

NO. 048

"Bring your parachute!"

Former Congressman and Vietnam Fighter Ace, Randy "Duke" Cunningham, was at a fundraiser for former Congressman Duncan Hunter, Sr. along with General Chuck Yeager.

Duke: "When I joined the American Fighter Aces Association, I was a bit shy and in awe of you, General Yeager, but now, I'm a bit more confident. Meet me tomorrow at 30,000 feet."

General Yeager immediately quipped: "Bring your parachute!"

General Chuck Yeager F-4 Phantom
(Both "Duke" & Yeager flew them in the Vietnam War)
(U.S. Air Force)

NO. 049

"Just to show I wasn't so Sierra Hotel (Sh– Hot); I was shot down the next day."

During World War II, Flight Officer Yeager shot down his first two enemy aircraft on March 4, 1944, (receiving credit for only one) while escorting a bomber group on the first American daylight raid to Berlin.

The very next day on a bombing run to Bordeaux, Yeager was shot down. "Sierra Hotel" is phonetic in aviation parlance for a fighter pilot's unprintable expression that means exceptionally great or wonderful.

NO. 050

"There ain't a German in the world can catch a West Virginian in the woods."

As a kid, young Charles Yeager learned to hunt and fish by stealthily stalking his prey. He used to explore the woods, swing from tree to tree, hike up the creek to Grandpa Yeager's house, and more. He also had Cherokee Indian blood and had taught himself to walk quietly in the woods. These talents were especially useful after he was shot down; they helped him successfully evade Germans huntin' for him.

NO. 051

"The French Underground hid me in the cathouses."

This was one of Yeager's answers to how he avoided capture by the Germans after he was shot down during World War II.

Chuck Yeager: "I was the first in my group to make it back after being shot down. The guys asked how I escaped the Germans. It wasn't true but it was funny."

NO. 052

"A French farmer ain't no match against a hungry hillbilly."

If the French farmer was foe, not friend, Yeager would have bested him. Fortunately, Flight Officer Yeager didn't have to do this. When Yeager was shot down during World War II, he had been trained to find poor folks— they would be more likely to help. He did (find the poor folks) and they (the poor farmers) did (help him). The farmers' children became great friends with Chuck & Victoria Yeager later in life.

NO. 053

"The one that kills the best with the least exposure to me."

"Whatever airplane got me behind the enemy first."

These were some of Yeager's responses to when someone would ask what was his favorite airplane.

NO. 054

"Depends on the mission."

This was another of Yeager's answers when asked what was his favorite airplane.

General Chuck Yeager flying an F-15E
(Artwork by Stu Shepard)

NO. 055

"It's not the plane, it's the pilot."
"It's not the machine, it's the man."

Yeager showed the difference between a better plane vs. a better pilot.

Some people get a little silly with this one, arguing an F-15E vs. a Cessna 150. Even so— please see the following story:

At the Edwards AFB, California 2005 air show, General Yeager flew a P-51 Mustang (a propeller airplane) on the wing of one of the U.S. Air Force's (USAF) newest jets, an F-22. The USAF wanted to show how slowly a stealthy Mach 2 jet, the F-22, could fly and then how quickly it could speed up especially in contrast to the 62-year-old World War II propeller fighter, the P-51 Mustang.

At the designated time, the P-51 Mustang and the F-22 did slow flight together, then cobbed it (went at full throttle). General Yeager in the P-51 Mustang took off, flying past the audience way ahead of the F-22. (General Yeager knew a jet needs time for the engine to spool up to speed up; a propeller plane does not.) The Air Force brass was not happy that their newest "baby," the F-22, was shown up by a 62-year-old World War II propeller airplane (and an 82-year-old pilot!)

F-22 with P-51 piloted by General Chuck Yeager, on its wing.
October 2005
(Courtesy of Stu Shepherd)

General Chuck Yeager flying P-51

NO. 056

On 9/11:

"It's no different than (World War II) Japanese kamikazes. Now people know what US pilots were dealing with in the Pacific during World War II."

NO. 057

"Me, he's dead."

A fan tweeted a question to General Yeager: "Who was a better pilot, Yeager or Eddie Rickenbacker." General Yeager's reply? "Me. Rickenbacker is dead." General Yeager was the ultimate pragmatist.

NO. 058

"Twenty-one (21) of the thirty (30) guys I went over with were shot down or killed."

Many guys approached General Yeager and said they wished they had been a fighter pilot in World War II. Even friend Carroll Shelby (famous race car driver and car designer, Shelby Mustang), who was an enlisted pilot like Yeager but, unlike Yeager, stayed stateside during World War II, wistfully told Chuck he wished he had fought in combat.

General Yeager's response was always: "Twenty-one (21) of the thirty (30) guys I went over with (to England for combat in Europe during World War II) didn't make it back (including his best friend Mac McKee)."

That got the wishful thinkers' attention. There's no glamour in war.

NO. 059

"You just hope you wake up before he does."

General Yeager was talking about dogfighting; turning so tight you pull about five G's (5x the normal pull of earth's gravity wherein your body feels five times heavier than usual which makes it harder for the heart to pump blood to your brain) and you black out. The guy chasing you also blacks out. "You just hope you wake up before he does."

NO. 060

"Sounds like a couple of active people in a waterbed: whole lotta sloshing going on."

General Yeager, on testing water G suits, really an anti-g suit designed to prevent blackouts such as described in the previous Chuck Yeager-ism, during World War II: "Once you got in the airplane, the crew chief would open the top nipples on the water G suit and fill them up with water. By the time you had flown an hour into Europe, the water had pooled by your ankles, and when you kicked the rudder (to turn); it sounded like a couple of active people in a waterbed.

(In other words: Not successful.).

Chuck Yeager: "Getting out of the P-51 Mustang was also a challenge after a long day of combat. You lifted each leg out of the cockpit. Then, you waddled out on the wing. The crew chief then opened the nipples at the bottom of the water G-suit causing two streams of water to pour out. After coffee, the subsequent 8-hour mission, and the power of suggestion; very quickly, there were three streams of liquid pouring over the side of the wing."

NO. 061

"Uncle Sam will give you all the flying and training you want... if you're willing to bleed a little bit."

NO. 062

On drones or unmanned vehicles, in combat:

"Any time a pilot doesn't have to bleed, it's a good thing."

The Air Force Academy had a leadership seminar. General Yeager was one of the speakers. The auditorium was packed including the balcony. They had never seen it this full with standing room only.

During the "Question and Answer" period, a student asked what General Yeager thought of drones or UAVs (unmanned aerial vehicles). The students expected General Yeager to disparage UAVs and support manned vehicles with pilots, especially fighter pilots. As Victoria Yeager was repeating the question, she thought, "They are not going to like this answer." And they didn't. Most students wanted to be fighter pilot jocks.

NO. 063

"A fighter pilot's breakfast: a coffee, a puke, and takeoff."

It was a joke— alluding to how much the guys drank and partied.

In reality, only once did that happen. They were told at Edwards AFB, California that they weren't going to be flying the next day, so they threw a party. Captain Yeager's father was visiting at the time.

The next morning, Captain Yeager drank some coffee and puked. His father said, "Son, is this how you always behave before you fly?"

X-1 above Rogers Dry Lake, Edwards AFB, CA (1940's)
(U.S. Air Force)

Chapter 5:

FLIGHT TEST: BREAKING THE SOUND BARRIER

NO. 064

"We didn't know if we could break the sound barrier, but it was our duty to try. That's the way I looked at it."

NO. 065

"You concentrate on what you are doing, to do the best job you can, stay out of serious situations. And that's the way the X-1 was. "

NO. O66

"It's not bragging if you can actually do it."

"It's not bragging if you can back it up with results!"

When General Yeager said he broke the sound barrier—he was the first to fly faster than the speed of sound at a time many thought the plane and pilot would blow apart into many tiny pieces—he was not bragging. He actually did it, one of the most dangerous and significant advances in aviation.

Captain Chuck Yeager October 14, 1947,
in X-1 cockpit after breaking the sound barrier.
(Courtesy of General Charles E. "Chuck" & Victoria Yeager)

NO. 067

"It wasn't that the X-1 would kill you; it was the *systems* in the X-1 that would kill you."

NO. 068

"The great ughknown."

"Later, I realized the real barrier wasn't in the sky, but in our knowledge and experience of supersonic flight."

This was a play on "the great unknown." At the time, what was beyond the sound barrier was unknown or ughknown.

NO. 069

"Just before you break through the sound barrier, the cockpit shakes the most."

Chuck Yeager: "Leveling off at 42,000 feet, I had thirty percent of my fuel, so I turned on rocket chamber three and immediately reached .96 Mach. I noticed that the faster I got, the smoother the ride. Suddenly the Mach needle began to fluctuate. It went up to .965 Mach—then tipped right off the scale...

We were flying supersonic. And it was as smooth as a baby's bottom; Grandma could be sitting up there sipping lemonade."

*X-1 after breaking the sound barrier
(Artwork by Stu Shepherd)*

NO. 070

"This Machmeter is all screwy."

Chuck Yeager radioed this the moment he flew past the sound barrier and the Machmeter showed it. The flight was confidential so this was code letting Jack Ridley, X-1 flight engineer, know they had accomplished what the "ol' man" (Colonel Albert "Al" Boyd, the father of USAF flight testing, later Major General Al Boyd) had sent them out to do: get past the sound barrier, fly above Mach 1, the speed of sound.

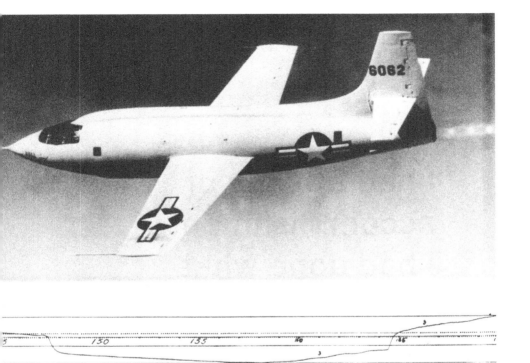

HISTORIC FIRST RECORDED "MACH JUMP", XS-1, OCT.14,1947

Captain Chuck Yeager flying X-1
nanoseconds after he exceeded Mach 1.
(Photo by Bob Hoover, flying chase, U.S. Air Force)

NO. 071

"I had a sense of accomplishment. I had done what the ol' man had sent me out to do."

This was Yeager's serious answer on being asked what it was like to break the sound barrier. The "ol' man" was Colonel Al Boyd, later Major General Albert Boyd. Captain Yeager did not risk his neck for money, fame, or glory which are fleeting.

a. Corollary: "It will never replace sex."

This was Yeager's answer on being asked by David Letterman on his late-night talk show what it was like to break the sound barrier.

David responded in jest, "So, *that* was the purpose of the experiment!"

General Chuck Yeager with David Letterman 1985
(Courtesy of Late Night with David Letterman)

NO. 072

"I was always afraid of dying. Always. It was my fear that made me learn everything I could about my airplane and my emergency equipment and kept me flying respectful of my machine and always alert in the cockpit."

NO. 073

"How can I bust my butt; how can I prevent it?"

"Never wait for trouble."

"If it can, it will… (go wrong)."

One should figure out how to prevent what could go wrong before anything does go wrong.

Captain Yeager was flying a virtual volatile bomb when he was flying the X-1. His Commanding Officer whom he admired and respected greatly wanted him to go through a barrier, the sound barrier, in this volatile bomb. Captain Yeager, to minimize the extreme risk, (people were being killed attempting it) would think, "What could go wrong; how can I prevent it?" Then, he'd try to fix, contain, or minimize what could go wrong before it did.

One such fix was installing redundancies. If Yeager lost his electrical system after he was dropped in the Bell X-1 from the B-29; he had no way of getting rid of the fuel, which was extremely flammable, volatile liquid oxygen. The landing gear was not stressed for the heavy load of a fully fueled plane. If he landed with a full load, the landing gear would collapse and the plane would explode.

For this reason, Yeager rigged a redundancy, a back-up manual release, for the fuel. He must have been clairvoyant, for the very next flight, his electrical system did go out. He tried the manual switch. He couldn't communicate with the chase plane because the radios worked on electricity. Thus, he had no way of knowing if the fuel was being dumped or not.

So every 1000 feet, he checked his stall speed, and it was lower than before, which meant he was losing fuel.

Still, when he landed, hne proverbially held his breath. And... he was fine. His redundancy method had worked. He had figured out how he could bust his butt and had prevented it.

NO. 074

"Yes, Sir, but I ain't in the Navy."

Yeager was being chewed out by a Navy admiral after stealing the Navy's thunder with an unscheduled runway takeoff in the X-1. The Navy admiral roared, "If you were in the Navy, I'd have you hung from the yard arm!"

Yeager's reply: "Yes, Sir. But I ain't in the Navy."

Captain Chuck Yeager with X-1 Glamorous Glennis
(U.S. Air Force)

NO. 075

Yeager:

"Ah, Ridley, there ain't nothing in there that can burn."

Ridley: "The hell there AIN'T; I'M in here."

Jack Ridley, Yeager's flight engineer on the X-1 and good friend, finally got his chance to fly the X-1 after Yeager had broken the sound barrier. Yeager flew chase. Ridley, in a panic, radioed, "Chuck, Chuck! There's a fire warning light in here!"

Yeager, who was used to seeing a fire warning light every time he flew the X-1, laconically replied, "Ah, hell, Ridley, there ain't nothing in there that can burn."

To which Ridley exclaimed, "The hell there AIN'T. I'M in here!"

Chuck Yeager & Jack Ridley 1947,
in front of X-1 strapped to B-29 ready for flight
(U.S. Air Force)

Major Chuck Yeager with F-86 (U.S. Air Force)

Colonel Chuck Yeager in F-100 (U.S. Air Force)

Chapter 6
MORE FLIGHT TESTING

NO. 076

"Know your egress systems better than the people who made (manufactured) them."

*Colonel Chuck Yeager piloting NF-104,
1963 (U.S. Air Force)*

It was only Yeager's thorough knowledge of his egress systems and airplane capabilities that saved his life many times. The most striking example is his NF-104 incident.

Colonel Yeager was flying the NF-104 for two reasons: altitude record (to eventually fly into space) and weightlessness, to give the future astronauts a feel for weightlessness, fewer to no pulls of gravity in space.

The NF-104 thrusters failed, so Yeager came back into the atmosphere tail first and ended up in a flat spin. He rode it down approximately 100,000 feet, trying every which way to get the plane out of the spin.

With the chase pilot frantically, constantly yelling at Yeager the entire 100,000' flat spin descent, to eject; Yeager remained calm and at 5,000-6,000 feet, under which is the safest altitude to eject, Yeager punched out. When he ejected, Yeager was going up as fast as the plane was going down (100 mph), so he was suspended in the air long enough for the rocket seat to get tangled in the parachute shroud lines. The rocket seat then came crashing down and the propellent hit his face mask, setting it on fire.

Yeager knew his egress systems better than the manufacturers. He knew he had to get the visor of his helmet up because that would stop the 100 percent oxygen airflow that was fueling the fire burning his face.

After he did so, he calmly, but desperately, kept scooping in air with his left hand to breathe fresh air, get oxygen and clear the smoke from his lungs.

When he landed, his shroud lines (ropes holding his harness to his parachute) were threadbare, burnt almost completely through. Yeager got his helmet off without help (unheard of). His fingers on his left hand and the left side of his face were severely burnt. His face was also somewhat bloody. The flight surgeon thought Yeager had lost his eye, but the blood had seared over it and protected it.

He would not have lived through that and been able to recover to flight status in a month had he not known his egress systems better than the folks who designed and manufactured them.

Colonel Yeager remained calm throughout the whole ordeal and remarkably remembered and conveyed each and every detail of the entire event in a debriefing.

NO. 077

When asked how to recover an F-104 from a flat spin, General Yeager answered:

"If you find out, let me know."

Yeager did all the flying in *The Right Stuff* movie except one time. The production team asked him to re-enact his NF-104 incident where his thrusters failed as he re-entered the atmosphere. This caused the NF-104 to re-enter tail first and then, enter into a flat spin out of which Yeager could not get the plane, so he eventually punched out. His rocket seat got caught in the shroud lines, burning them, then fell and hit his facemask setting it on fire. (Please see prior Yeager-ism.)

His response to the production team was a flat, "No. Whoever tries that is going to kill himself."

So, the production team got another pilot and...Yeager was right, the new pilot and plane augured in.

NF-104 crash December 10, 1963: Yeager ejected in time

NO. 078

"It can ruin your whole day."

Yeager casually said this to David Letterman after describing the NF-104 incident where he had to bail out; the rocket seat hit his face mask and set his face on fire. "It can ruin your whole day." (Please see prior two Yeager-isms for a more detailed description.)

General Chuck Yeager with David Letterman, 1985
(Courtesy of Late Night with David Letterman)

a. Corollary: "It was nothin'."

Yeager explains, after plummeting down toward earth 100,000 feet in a flat spin in the NF-104, "So, I took it down to 5,000 feet and punched out." A Yeagerian shrug then, "It was nothin'."

SR-71
(Artwork by Stu Shepherd)

b. Corollary: "It's okay."

At a seminar for military pilots, this was Yeager's matter-of-fact, simple response when someone asked him what he thought of the SR-71, the coolest looking, stunning and very advanced (at that time) jet airplane, which he had just flown the week before.

c. Corollary: "And that's bad."

This is how Chuck Yeager tells this story: "While training for combat in World War II in Wyoming, my (P-39) plane's engine froze. I parachuted out and landed in a field, unconscious at first. I had broken my back. 'And that's bad.' A farmer put me on his mule which was not comfortable, to say the least, but he brought me to safety."

The rest of the story is that the doctors told Yeager he wouldn't walk again. Yeager had a seven-letter, two-syllable word that starts with a "B" for them. And as Yeager said, "I'm not a quitter!" Not only did Yeager walk again, but he also became a fighter ace and test pilot extraordinaire.

P-39 (Artwork by Stu Shepherd)

NO. 079

"It's just like practicing bleeding. Man, when the time comes, you're going to do it, you know. No question."

This was in response to the question: "General Yeager, how do you bail out of an airplane without practicing?"

a. Corollary:

In response to the question, "Did you practice parachuting before you had to bail out?" and "Why not?";

General Yeager replied, "No, for the same reason I never practiced dying, either."

NO. 080

"I've been closer to heaven than you have."

Reverend Robert Schuler of the famed Crystal Cathedral in Orange County, California, which used to have real, live camels when it re-enacted the original Christmas day, had asked General Yeager if he was afraid when he was test flying new airplanes, stretching the envelope, going to 118,000 feet long before anyone had gone to the moon. Yeager replied, "No, I wasn't afraid. You know, Reverend Schuler, I've been closer to heaven than you have."

Colonel Chuck Yeager flew the NF-104 to over 118,000'
(Artwork by Stu Shepherd)

NO. 081

"By the time I leveled out, I was so high I could've shaken hands with Lord Jesus!"

Colonel Yeager said this after flying the NF-104 to over 118,000'.

NO. 082

"I don't have time to be afraid; I have to fix the problem."

This was Chuck Yeager's second reply to Reverend Robert Schuler of the famed California Crystal Cathedral when the reverend pressed the question a second time: Wasn't General Yeager afraid when he was test flying new airplanes?

NO. 083

"You can pray all the way down into a smokin' hole. I have to fix the problem."

When asked: "When things go very wrong, do you ever pray?" Chuck replied: "No, I'm usually kinda busy. Sure, you can pray all the way down into a smokin' hole. I have to fix the problem."

Other Chuck Yeager responses:

"It's really difficult for fanatic churchgoers to understand God can't help me. I'm the only one who can help me.

"I really didn't have apprehension because it doesn't do a damn bit of good. It's like religious people say: 'When you get into trouble in an airplane, don't you pray?'

"My answer: 'No, God can't help me. I've got to help myself.' And that's basically the way you look at it."

General Yeager had to fix the problem quickly many times. One such time occurred in 1953 when his airplane, the X1-A, was spinning out of control on all three axes doing three snap rolls per second. In addition, he was knocked out for a few seconds. When he came to, he recognized an inverted spin, kicked it into a regular spin, stopped the spin, recovered, and landed the airplane. Even all his self-proclaimed rivals said Yeager was the only one who could have saved that plane and himself that day.

Major Chuck Yeager with X-1A 1953 (U.S. Air Force)

NO. 084

"You don't worry about the outcome. If you die, you don't know anything about it anyway, so you just wipe it out of your mind"

Various versions:

"I don't let fear get in the way of accomplishing the mission."

"You learn to discipline yourself and concentrate on what you're doing so you're not scared, and you don't worry about the outcome." –Johnny Carson Show

Many religions preach: "Be present." Chuck Yeager was that and more, especially in a dangerous situation. He didn't waste time worrying or letting fear get in the way of fixing the problem. As he was spinning on all three axes in the X-1A, (three snap rolls per second) he tried different actions in sequence to save himself and the airplane. And by doing so, succeeded in saving both himself and his airplane to fly another day.

Major Chuck Yeager in X-1A 1953 (U.S. Air Force)

MORE FLIGHT TESTING | 121

Question: "Were you ever scared doing test flights? (Or combat?)"

Chuck Yeager's answers:

"Constantly. But I didn't let it get in the way. What good does it do to be afraid? It doesn't help anything. You better try and figure out what's happening and correct it."

"You can get yourself into a position where it's impossible to get out. Well, obviously you're going to die then. If you die, you don't know anything about it anyway, so you just wipe it out of your mind and concentrate on what you're doing."

"I think we learn real quick: you obviously don't waste time thinking about something over which you have no control, so you put it out of your mind and concentrate on what you're doing and stay out of that region."

NO. 085

"The engineers call it triaxial rotation. I call it hell."

Major Chuck Yeager in X-1A exceeded Mach 2 (Mach 2.44) 1953
(U.S. Air Force)

NO. 086

"Why would you jump out of a perfectly good airplane?"

In his flying career, General Yeager had three more take-offs than landings. Each time he had to punch or jump out of his damaged aircraft, he sustained serious injuries. To guys and gals that did it for fun, he'd ask them this: "Why would you jump out of a perfectly good airplane?"

NO. 087

"How did you know?"

Pancho Barnes, an accomplished pilot and adventurer herself, who owned a ranch/bar/motel just off Muroc, later Edwards, AFB, had complained about the test pilots buzzing her place after takeoff. The only person whom she didn't mind was Yeager. She knew he was safe.

Pancho Barnes, aviatrix,
Happy Bottom Riding Club, & Chuck Yeager
(Courtesy of Estate of Pancho Barnes)

One morning Yeager and another guy buzzed Pancho's. When they returned, Yeager got messages to report to Colonel Boyd's office immediately and from Pancho Barnes to call her before Yeager did anything else. Pancho alerted Yeager that Colonel Boyd had been sleeping in one of her motel rooms with one of her gals, not his wife, that morning.

Yeager and the other pilot then went to Colonel Boyd's office.

Colonel Boyd growled: "I gave you a direct order not to buzz Pancho's. And you defied that order this morning!"

Yeager figured, 'What the hell— I can't be in any worse trouble,' so he asked, "Sir, how did you know?"

Colonel Boyd glared at him for a full minute and eventually roared: "GET OUT!"

(Courtesy of Estate of Pancho Barnes)

NO. 088

"Never let them name a street after you at Edwards."

General Yeager was the first and only living pilot after whom they named a street at Edwards AFB, CA. Before and after that, streets were named only for those who had augured in. When the Commander told Yeager Edwards AFB was going to name a street after him, Yeager's response was a seven-letter, two-syllable word starting with a "B", making it abundantly clear they had better not. But they did: "Yeager Boulevard".

Chuck Yeager statue in front of Chuck Yeager Boulevard,
Edwards AFB, California 2006
(Courtesy of Robert Tarn)

NO. 089

"Never get yourself
into a position where
they have to bring
in a pathologist to
identify you."

NO. 090

"You don't concentrate on risks. You concentrate on results. No risk is too great to prevent the necessary job from getting done."

"I evaluated the rewards against the risk."

NO. 091

"Everyone's got a job to do, Son."

An Air Force Academy graduate, a captain, flying with General Yeager, asked General Yeager why he was carrying his own gear out to the airplane. This was General Yeager's response.

*General Chuck Yeager after his last active duty flight
F-4C Phantom, Feb 25, 1975 (U.S. Air Force)*

Chapter 7
NASA

NO. 092

"In 1966, NASA took over in space, and it has been a bureaucratic mess ever since."

General Yeager did praise NASA's unmanned exploration of space, especially Mars, and said they should stick to that. He also praised the astronauts who never forgot where they came from; especially those from the U.S. Air Force.

NO. 093

"Nah! I didn't want to wipe the monkey crap off the seat before I sat down."

On television, veteran news anchorman extraordinaire Walter Cronkite asked General Yeager if he had wanted to be an astronaut. The above was Yeager's answer.

NO. 094

"Speed is relative. Now you've got guys in space vehicles smokin' along at 1000s of miles an hour."

NO. 095

"They Got Their Publicity."

In January 1986, President Ronald Reagan wisely appointed General Chuck Yeager to the Challenger Accident Board.

General Chuck Yeager (U.S. Air Force)

General Yeager was criticized by some of the other board members after he showed up for only two days and departed.

Yeager departed because even before the board convened, they (and everyone) already knew the cause of the accident—too cold, and the O-rings had frozen.

Yeager didn't want to waste his time on food and drink and staying in a luxury hotel on the government's dime after the mission was accomplished. The others were afraid Yeager's leaving would expose the real reason the rest stayed an extra week or more.

As General Yeager said, "NASA had to keep putting off the launch day after day due to the cold weather and warnings regarding the O-rings. After six long days, NASA noticed the press was getting bored and leaving. So, NASA insisted on the launch."

And the shuttle blew up.

Yeager continued dryly, "They got their publicity."

*Challenger blowing up right after launch January 28, 1986
(NASA)*

NO. 096

"All Cause Accident"

Long before the Challenger accident, General Yeager, in his last assignment in the U.S. Air Force, was Director of Safety; he investigated all U.S. Air Force accidents from 1973 to 1975.

Prior to Yeager assuming command as Director of Safety, the policy regarding accident investigations historically had been to determine the primary cause and the secondary causes.

The U.S. Air Force would fix the primary cause but not the secondary causes. Next would be an accident where one of the secondary causes had become the primary cause and only then would it get fixed.

So General Yeager changed the protocol of accident investigation reports from one primary cause and the secondary causes to an "All Cause Accident".

In this way, all the causes would get fixed without waiting for another accident.

Apparently, NASA did not follow this brilliant and simple change implemented by General Chuck Yeager and the U.S. Air Force.

Allegedly NASA was aware of approximately over 35 issues and only corrected 33; some of the ones they did not correct were the tiles.

Columbia Shuttle disintegrating upon reentry , February 1, 2003
(Used with permission from Dr. Scott Lieberman)

And the Columbia blew up upon re-entry due to the tile issues. NASA's waste of human life truly angered General Yeager.

Remembrance Day Arlington National Cemetery
February 1, 2013, (NASA/Bill Ingalis)

However, the civilian world followed General Yeager's protocol and so General Yeager saved 10s of millions of lives.

Chapter 8
HOMESPUN QUIPS

NO. 097

"Son, you oughta get a little closer to your razor when you shave."

General Yeager was not a fan of beards. You couldn't get a good seal on your oxygen mask with facial hair so you could be prone to hypoxia. If one of the pilots in a flight of four, eight, 16, or 64, is not acting at 100 percent, he jeopardizes everyone else in the flight. Plus, being in the military, General Yeager was used to grooming standards.

NO. 098

On Golf:

"I'm not old enough to play golf and I never will be."

At Edwards AFB, many of the generals and colonels would play golf, riding from one hole to the next in their golf cart, getting very little to no exercise. When Yeager had time off, he'd go huntin' or fishin' or hiking into the High Sierra. Many of those golfers would retire and die shortly thereafter. Yeager lived to almost ninety-eight.

NO. 099

"Bet he doesn't have the guts to do that again!"

(bug splat on the window)

NO. 100

"If a toad had wings, it wouldn't bump its a$$ every time it jumped."

(In response to "If only...")

NO. 101

"I don't buy green bananas. I'm afraid they won't get ripe before I die."

Chapter 9
BONUS

NO. 102

"Practice your retirement before you retire."

Lots of people retire and then don't know what to do with themselves and often wish they hadn't retired.

NO. 103

On someone else driving too fast:

"OK, Barney Oldfield, (well-known racecar driver), if I'm going to die, I wanna kill myself."

Barney Oldfield was a great racecar driver in his day. In the first two decades of the 20th century, his name was synonymous with speed. Yeager would say this to drivers who were driving too fast or driving too close to another vehicle while Yeager was a passenger.

Chuck Yeager at the Indy 500

NO. 104

"There is no 'THE' in my name."

Yeager would respond with this to people who asked, "Are you THE Chuck Yeager?"

NO. 105

"How do I KNOW who you THINK I am?!"

This was in response to a stranger at the airport asking: "Are you who I think you are?"

NO. 106

Fan accosting General Yeager: "I read your book!"

Yeager:

"Good. Then we won't have to talk."

NO. 107

"Never trust a skinny cook."

NO. 108

"You going on furlough?"

"You obviously don't miss too many meals."

Yeager would say the first one to anyone who had piled a meal high on their plate or was eating a lot.

And he'd say the second one to someone who fit the bill.

NO. 109

"Hard to watch yourself age 70 years in 26 minutes."

General Yeager had just watched, with the audience, a 26-minute documentary on his life before giving a talk and doing a question and answer session.

NO. 110

"Now it takes me all night to do what I used to do all night!"

(Courtesy of the Oak Ridge Boys)

NO. 111

"When you stick your neck out, you get bit every once in a while."

NO. 112

"I didn't take you to raise. If I did, I'd have better clothes on you."

NO. 113

"Do you know the definition of a slow person?"

When someone would ask the same question in the same thread, Yeager would respond with,

"You know the definition of a slow person? A slow person is someone running around introducing himself when everyone else is already shacked up."

NO. 114

"Do you know what a sexual intellectual is?"

Chuck Yeager: "An F-ing know-it-all!"

NO. 115

"What's it gonna cost me?"

The Oak Ridge Boys had heard the World War II 357th Fighter Group, of which General Chuck Yeager was a member, was having their reunion in Myrtle Beach, SC. The Boys invited General Yeager to bring his group to their show that night.

General Yeager's response was: "What's it gonna cost me?"

They replied, "No, Sir, as our guest." (And thus began a 30-year friendship.)

(Courtesy of the Oak Ridge Boys)

NO. 116

"Nobody likes a smarta$$"

NO. 117

"Don't bring me problems, bring me solutions."

NO. 118

"Looks like the box it came in."

This was regarding some types of cars.

NO. 119

When asked what he thought of Nascar:

"Professional fender benders."

NO. 120

"You can't eat the horns."

Most folks like to hunt record-size elk or deer. Those records are measured by the antlers. But Chuck Yeager wasn't most folks—he ate or fed others what he hunted. For this reason, he hunted yearling cow elk— tender meat, much better than an "old, dead bull elk" with bigger antlers. General Yeager also preferred culling.

Chuck Yeager, age 89, culled a wildebeest in South Africa to feed a local tribe in 2010 (with Victoria Yeager). (Courtesy of Joe da Silva)

NO. 121

"The Good Lord made only so many perfect heads. The rest he covered with hair."

NO. 122

"This is my week for girls."

President George H.W. Bush, affectionately known by Chuck & Victoria Yeager as "Daddy Bush", asked General Yeager to campaign with him in 1988. General Yeager would get a standing ovation, then he'd speak for a little while and introduce Daddy Bush. Daddy Bush would get up to speak. No standing ovation; just polite clapping. Daddy Bush told Chuck, "You're a hard act to follow!"

The first time, Daddy Bush asked Chuck, "You want to take a nap? Every day at 5 pm, I take a half-hour nap. Come on!"

General Yeager, laughing, told the rest of the story: "I replied, 'Mr. Vice President, this is my week for girls, Sir!'

"We went to Daddy Bush's suite, into the bedroom where there were two single beds. Daddy Bush lay down on one of the beds. When I hesitated, he pointed to the other bed and ordered, 'Lie down.'

"I said, 'Yes, sir,' and laid down as directed; but I kept one eye open on him the whole time."

NO. 123

"Take-offs are optional, landings are mandatory."

General Yeager had three more take-offs than landings with his airplane.

One: In October 1943, while training for combat, Yeager's P-39 engine froze. Yeager and his airplane parted company and he parachuted out.

Two: In March 1944, flying a P-51B, Yeager was shot down over France during World War II. He parachuted out.

Three: In December 1963, Yeager ejected out of the NF-104 after he could not get it out of a flat spin.

Chapter 10
FINAL NOTE

NO. 124

"I tell things the way I remember them, and that's not necessarily the way they happened."

NO. 125

In response to the question, "If you had to do it all over again, would you do it differently?:

"No. That's speculation."

a. Corollary: "No regrets."

Chuck Yeager: "Doesn't do you any good."

NO. 126

"It's classified."

General Yeager would give this answer when he didn't want to answer a question.

NO. 127

"I was at the right place at the right time."

This was his response when people asked how he had such a phenomenal career out of the hollers of West Virginia. He also said that explained others' great successes as well.

NO. 128

"The person I am is the sum total of the life I've lived."

NO. 129

"If I auger in tomorrow,
it won't be with a
frown on my face.
I've had a ball! "

NO. 130

"'What a ride!' This will be the last line of my obituary. Really."

NO. 131

"It'll be all right."

General Chuck Yeager flying P-51
[Courtesy of Colonel Pat Duffy USAF (ret.)]

Chuck Yeager's last military flight

ACKNOWLEDGEMENTS

Thank you to those who helped put this book together and in legible form and/or guided me through the process with great patience, in order of appearance: Jean Quinn, Bobbi Giudicelli, Jan Du Plain, Muriel Nellis, Elizabeth Ridley, Bryan Dougherty, Jonathan Metz, Tara Mayberry, Stu Shepherd, Lou D'Elia, Chris Patti.

Thank you to our friends and followers who reminded me of some of Chuck Yeager's quotes when I was in such a fog, I couldn't remember anything. A special thank you very much for our friendship, your kindness, patience, help, great sense of humor, courtesy, and honest opinions: Diana Duffy, Denise Forbes, Debi Young, Bob Tarn, Katherine Duffy, Joe & Nicole da Silva, Julie Clark, Dotty Duke, Glenna Smith, Mike Flynn.

READING LIST

Yeager, An Autobiography by Chuck Yeager & Leo Janos

Coming out next year: Working title: *Chuck YEAGER & me; Formation Flying & other great Adventures with America's Hero, the Right Stuff* by Victoria Yeager, Chuck Yeager's favorite wingman.

www.chuckyeager.com

ABOUT THE AUTHOR/ WINGMAN

VICTORIA YEAGER was born in Philadelphia, attended girls' school, has a BA from the University of Virginia, spending her junior year in Paris taking classes from the Sorbonne, Sorbonne Nouvelle, and the Institute of Political Science and has an MBA from Columbia University. She has consulted nonprofit and NGO companies all over the world advocating against human trafficking, hunger, and homelessness. She has helped educate indigenous people about nutrition, finances, and the prevention of alcoholism and drug abuse. She is also an actor, producer, director, and writer. She enjoys traveling, flying (taught by Chuck Yeager), horseback riding, huntin', fishing, sailing, bodysurfing, reading, trekking, whitewater rafting, and pickleball. In 2000, she met General Chuck Yeager on a hiking trail in the middle of nowhere. As her friend said, "Clearly, it was meant to be." Chuck and Victoria married in 2003. Victoria is thrilled and honoured to share the humor and wisdom of her late great husband, General Chuck Yeager.

Visiting Prince Malik Atta Muhammad Khan in Pakistan (2012)
Photo by General Chuck Yeager

General Chuck Yeager with B-2 (U.S. Air Force)

INDEX

* *Italics* are used to indicate illustrations.

A

N

O

P

R

Reagan, Ronald (U.S. President), xiv, 135

Redundancies, installing, 99–100

Remembrance Day, at Arlington National Cemetery, *138*

Retirement, *x, xii,* 30, 147

Rickenbacker, Eddie, 77

Ridley, Jack, vii, 94, 102

   with Yeager, Chuck, *103*

The Right Stuff, iv, v, xi, xiii, 48, 108, 181

Rocky Basin Lakes, 54

Rogers Dry Lake, *84*

S

Schuler, Robert, 113, 116

Shelby, Carroll, 78

Shelby Mustang, 78

"Sierra Hotel," 68

Smith's Ranch Lake, 42, *43*

Snowbirds, 6

Sound barrier, breaking of, xii, xiv, 30, 84, 85, 86, 88, *89,* 91, 92, *93,* 94, *95,* 96, 97, 99, 102, 104,

South Africa, culling in, *165*

Statues of Yeager, Chuck, 36, *37, 127*

Symington, Stuart (U.S. Air Force Secretary), 30

T

Tail End Charlie, 4

357th Fighter Group, 4, 160

Truman, Harry S, presentation of Collier Trophy to Yeager, 29–30, *30*

on touch and goes, 42
on triaxial rotations, 122
on UFO's, 56
on unsportsmanlike behavior, 65
on war, 78
on water G suits, 80
on toads, 143
on worrying, 119

Made in the USA
Coppell, TX
22 September 2022

83478434R00118